HISTORIC UNION CEMETERY

George H. Shafer at the reins of his horse-drawn hearse, Brentwood, 1905

Byron-Brentwood-Knightsen Union Cemetery District

Published by Byron Hot Springs, San Francisco, California

A COLLABORATION BY THE MEMBERS OF
THE EAST CONTRA COSTA HISTORICAL SOCIETY AND
THE BYRON-BRENTWOOD-KNIGHTSEN UNION CEMETERY DISTRICT

Originally Published: September 2003
Revised: November 2020

2003 Cemetery Tour Committee Members

Kathy Leighton
Sharon Marsh
Maureen Murray
Barbara Russell-Cambra

2020 Historic Union Cemetery Committee

Aurora Garcia, District Manager, Union Cemetery District
Patricia Howard, District Co-Manager, Union Cemetery District
Doreen Forlow, President, East Contra Costa Historical Society
Kathy Leighton, President Emeritus, East Contra Costa Historical Society and Original Author
Magdalena Northcut, Second Vice President, East Contra Costa Historical Society and Photographer
Carol A. Jensen, Member, East Contra Costa Historical Society and Editor

2020 Union Cemetery Board of Trustees

Patricia Bristow, President, term July 1, 2018 to December 31, 2022
Barbara Guise, Trustee, term January 1, 2010 to December 31, 2022
Deborah Spinola, Trustee, term October 22, 2019 to December 31, 2021

For additional copies or to arrange a docent tour, please contact the
Byron-Brentwood-Knightsen Union Cemetery District
11545 Brentwood Boulevard, Brentwood, CA 94513
Telephone (925) 634-4748
Website: www.unioncemeterydistrict.com

 Published by Byron Hot Springs, San Francisco, California
www.byronhotsprings.com

ISBN: 978-0-578-76599-0

Library of Congress Control Number: 2021935275

10 9 8 7 6 5 4 3

Copyright © 2020 The Byron-Brentwood-Knightsen Union Cemetery District. All rights reserved.

Images reproduced herein are Copyright © 2020 East Contra Costa Historical Society and may not be reproduced without specific, written permission by the Society. All rights reserved.

Disclaimer: All errors and Commissions are the responsibility of the
2020 Historic Union Cemetery Committee. We welcome your corrections.

Cover and interior design and composition by Leigh McLellan Design

UNION CEMETERY

"Articles of Incorporation were filed for the Union Cemetery Association of Point of Timber, Contra Costa County. It issues no capital stock. Its directors are J.T. Pearce, R.N McEntyre, A. Richardson, W.T. Grover, A.T. Taylor, George Fellows and Math Berlinger." According to the *Sacramento Daily Union*, Volume 7, Number 103, June 18, 1878, page 3 column 1.

Union Cemetery is one of only 256 California public cemetery districts. Districts are separate local governments, located mostly in rural areas or suburban areas that once were rural. They pay for their expenses through interment fees and a piece of local property tax revenue. Generally, only taxpayers or former taxpayers of the cemetery district and their families are eligible for burial. In the case of our Union Cemetery, only eligible parties from Byron, Brentwood, Knightsen, Bethel Island and Discovery Bay are eligible for interment. The term "Union" is a common descriptor used in naming cemeteries before and after the Civil War. "Union" does not specifically refer to the Union Army vs the Confederate Army. According to the Merriam-Webster Law Dictionary, "…union is a political unit constituting an organic whole formed usually from units which were previously governed separately (such as England and Scotland in 1707) and which have surrendered or delegated their principal powers to the government of the whole or to a newly created government (such as the U.S. in 1789)."[1] "Union" in this usage pertains to "unified" or "aggregate" or "together" as in a "more perfect union" as found in the preamble of the U.S. Constitution.[2]

Several months after the Cemetery's incorporation, the true operation of the Union Cemetery Association began when Colburn J. Preston, a pioneer of the Point of Timber area, sold four acres for $10 on November 1, 1878 to the Union Cemetery Association. Colburn, specified the acreage to be used as a cemetery. R. M. Jones surveyed and plotted the four-acre grounds in October 1868. Prior to this sale, burials occurred on private family properties or at the Point of Timber graveyard on the Sylvester Wills Ranch then located at present day Marsh Creek Road and Highway 4. Some residents objected to having a cemetery so close to Excelsior School. The area was also prone to flooding making it impossible to hold burials during the rainy season. An alternative for the growing community had to be found. Creation of the Union Cemetery Association and the Point of Timber Cemetery was the solution.

The Point of Timber district is located in the far eastern part of Contra Costa County between the Eden Plains district and present day Byron. Point of Timber was a vast cattle grazing and grain growing area. Farmers shipped their product initially out of Babbe's Landing on Dutch Slough and later Point of Timber Landing on Indian Slough. The district gains its name from the mile-wide strip of open oak woodland that ran from just east of the John Marsh stone house along the course

---

1. California Association of Public Cemeteries. "What You Should Know About California Public Cemetery Districts" http://capc.info. Accessed: October 5, 2020

2. *Merriam-Webster Law Dictionary,* Definition 2 B (1) https://www.merriam-webster.com/dictionary/union. Accessed September 21, 2020

of Kellogg Creek.[3] Creation of the landing along Indian Slough was a cooperative effort of Point of Timber district landholders under the leadership of Josiah Wills. Improving, deepening and connecting Indian Slough to Old River created a shipping port closer than Babbe's Landing for the Point of Timber grain farmers. Plus, no fees were payable to a third party when the landing is owned cooperatively by the local farmers.

Construction of the Tulare and San Pablo Railroad (Southern Pacific) in 1878 changed both the economic and social dynamics of the area. With the railroad came the Bethany, Byron and Brentwood railroad stations and around them grew these railroad transportation towns. The real estate rush was on for lots in these overnight towns providing grain storage and grain transportation to Port Costa grain wharves. The community of Point of Timber languished into obscurity. (See the map on p. 5.)

The hardy settlers at Point of Timber did all in their power to build up a law-abiding community, and accumulate fortunes for themselves. Alonzo Plumley came in 1851. So did Ferdinand Hoffman, who owned 920 acres of land; and J. S. Netherton was the third settler in Point of Timber. H. C. Gallagher and his wife, Amanda, J. E. Carey, J. F. Carey, A. Richardson, W. R. Wilder, C. J. Preston, D. Perkins, D. K. Berry, M. Berlinger, Thomas McCabe, J. P. McCabe, H. C. McCabe, George Cople, A. T. Taylor, J. Christensen, R. N. McEntyre, W. J. Cotes, J. B. Henderson, R. G. Dean, M. A. Walton, J. H. Baldwin and others were among the number who laid the foundation for this thriving community.[4] Most of these families are buried here at Union Cemetery

The deceased originally interred on the Wills' property were relocated to the new Cemetery which explains why some markers date before the Union Cemetery Association was established. The earliest headstone is for Margaret Easton (Unit 1, Lot 39) who passed at age ten in 1865. The second oldest grave is for Gallant Lee Veale (Unit 1, Lot 45) who passed at age one or two on November 22, 1867 and memorialized on her mother's gravestone. Five other graves date prior to the establishment of the cemetery as moved from private land or from the informal Wills

---

3. *Goodspeed Histories*, https://goodspeedhistories.com/query-union-cemeteries/ accessed September 20, 2020

Minute record book and original bylaws of the Union Cemetery Association

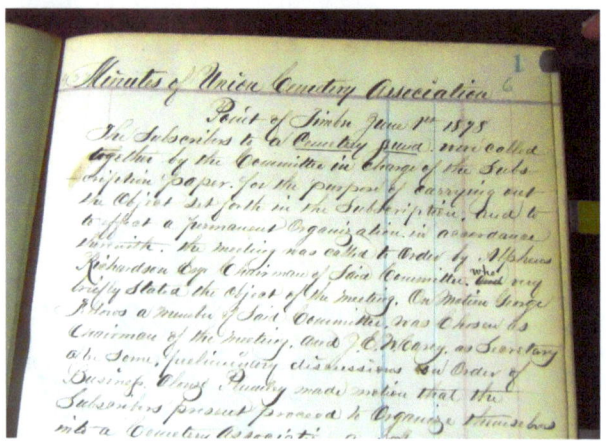

---

4. Hulaniski, Frederick J. *The History of Contra Costa County, California*, (Published by Elms Publishing Co., Inc. Berkeley, CA) 1917 p. 169

Ranch graveyard near the original Excelsior School. Marshal ("Marty") Benn (1878–1984) Unit 2, Lot 73, lived to be 106 years old and holds the distinction of the longest-lived person buried at Union Cemetery.

Additional land and modern upgrades to the facility have kept pace with the industry and community needs. The Cemetery Board of Trustees acquired an additional 2½ acres from Colburn Preston at $250.00 an acre in 1919.[5] A new ossuary and a two-sided columbarium were added in 2002 prompted by the increased incidence and preference for cremation. Cremated remains may now be interred with a relative, in-ground niches, in an underground vault (ossuary) or in an above ground vault (columbarium). Once considered controversial, memorial benches honoring the deceased are now acceptable.

The non-denominational, public Union Cemetery is now managed as of 1928 by the Byron-Brentwood-Knightsen Union Cemetery District developed under the California State Health and Safety Code. The Cemetery is taxpayer owned and only those living within the cemetery district or those having close relations buried at Union Cemetery may be buried there. The district includes those in the cemetery district name plus Bethel Island and Discovery Bay. Today there are over 4,000 individuals in graves, including cremated remains plus those interred in the "potters' field" in the ten-acre cemetery

The 2020 Cemetery District Board consists of President Patricia Bristow, Trustee Barbara Guise, and Trustee Deborah Spinola as appointed by the Contra Costa County Board of Supervisors.

---

5. Election of Officers by Cemetery Board, Antioch Ledger, *Brentwood News* Section, September 27, 1919

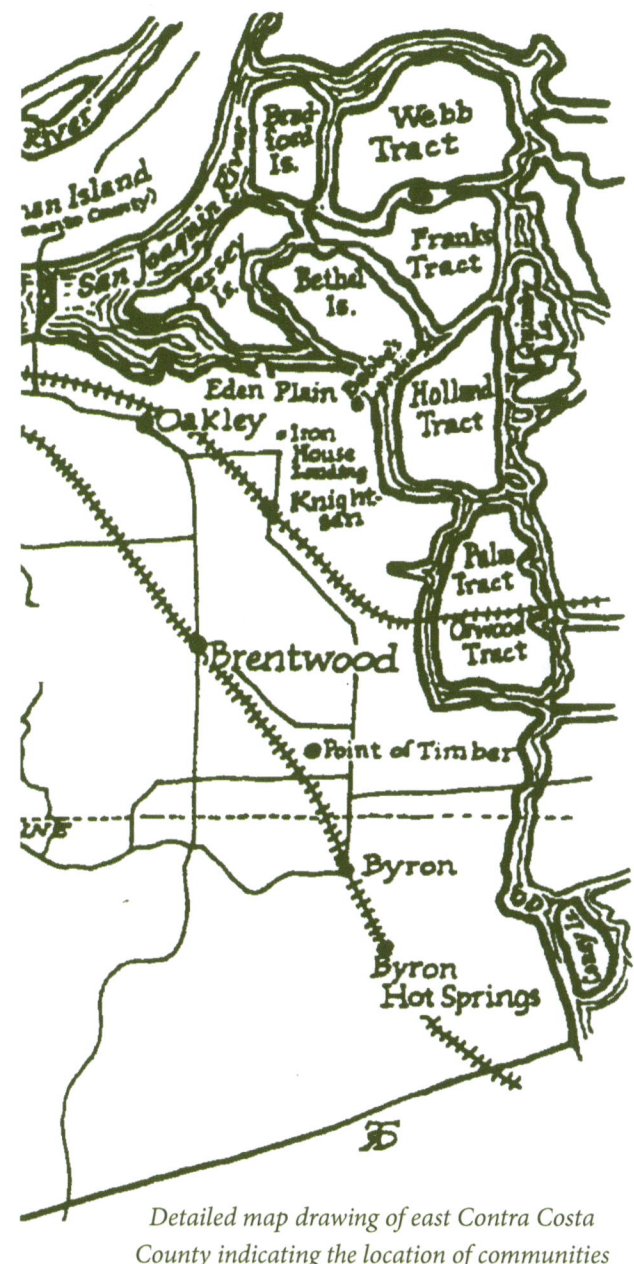

Detailed map drawing of east Contra Costa County indicating the location of communities mentioned in this book. Map is not to scale.[6]

The staff of the Cemetery is Aurora Garcia, District Manager, and Patricia Howard, District Co-Manager. Caretakers, David Garcia, Maintenance Foreman, and Hector Garcia, Groundskeeper, make sure the grounds always look their best.

---

6. Tatum, Robert D. *Old Times in Contra Costa County: A Journey to the Past* Pittsburg, CA: Highland Publishers.1993 p. 2

BRENTWOOD FUNERAL HOME

The first undertaking business in Brentwood was established in 1905 by George H. Shafer. His father's livery stable was the preparation room, and stands today on the original property on First Street. His funeral parlor was originally George and his wife, Martha's ("Pattie" or "Patty") home which consisted of the four- or five-room house that had been brought to Brentwood from Nortonville by Jack Norman. A chapel was added in 1931 to serve grieving families and friends. In 1934, a new funeral parlor was built replacing the old one. The renamed "Shafer Funeral Home" was sold to Frank Wiseman in 1947 but reverted to Shafer after two years.

In 1949, Roy and Alice Bartheld bought the business, changed the name to "The Brentwood Funeral Home" and renovated it into a modern facility. Local student, Patrick McHenry worked for Bartheld while attending elementary and high school. Upon graduation from Liberty Union High School, McHenry attended the University of the Pacific and the San Francisco College of Mortuary Science. McHenry returned to Brentwood and worked for Bartheld for seven years. In 1969, Roy and Alice Bartheld sold the business to Patrick and Donnalee McHenry, who operated the business together as" The Brentwood Funeral Home" until 1985 when Ray Glosser was hired as a second full-time director. In 1979, a fire in the mortuary necessitated a second renovation. Patrick McHenry sold the business in 1993 to the Loewen Group of Covington, Kentucky and remained as

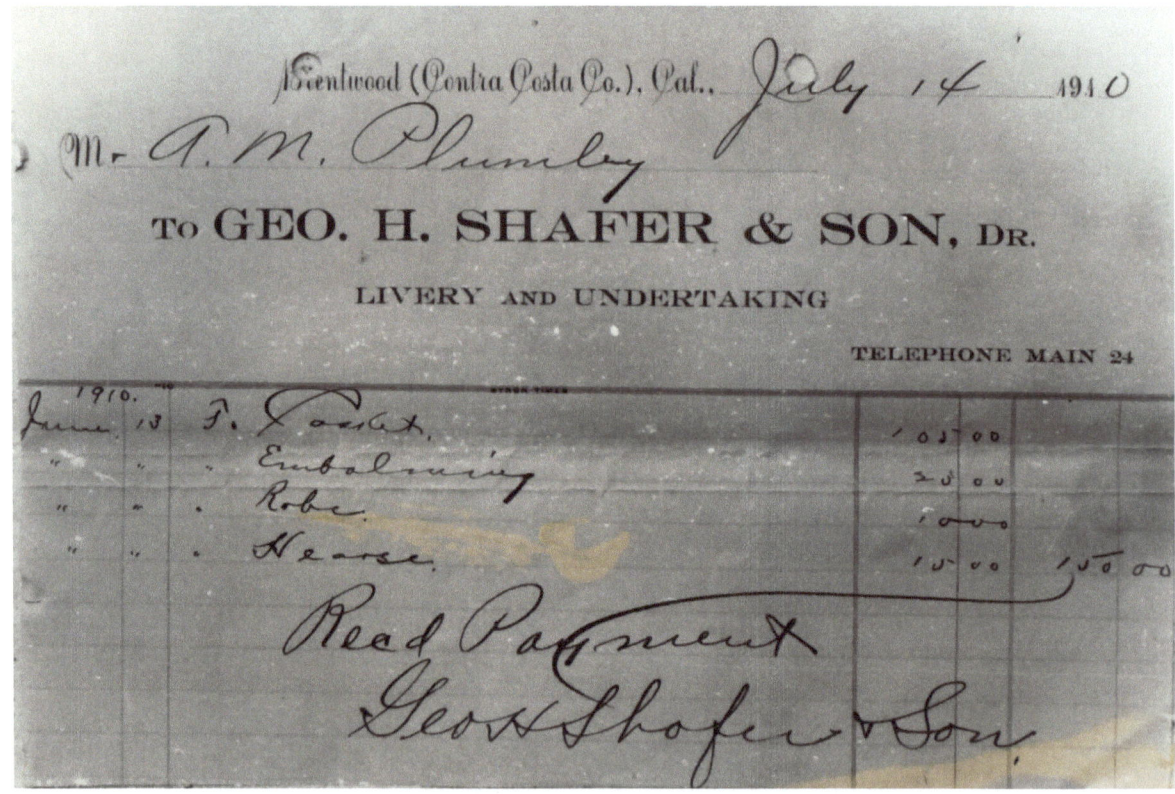

Business billhead from the George H. Shafer & Son, Brentwood, invoicing and acknowledging payment for undertaking services, July 14, 1910.

manager until his 1996 retirement. Ray Glosser continued his tenure until he retired in 2007.

The business subsequently sold to Service Corporation International but continues operations as the Brentwood Funeral Home. Today funeral and cremation services continue to be provided with dignity under the capable hands of Elise-Marie Surucu, Location Manager.

One of liveryman and undertaker George H. Shafer's horse-drawn hearses.

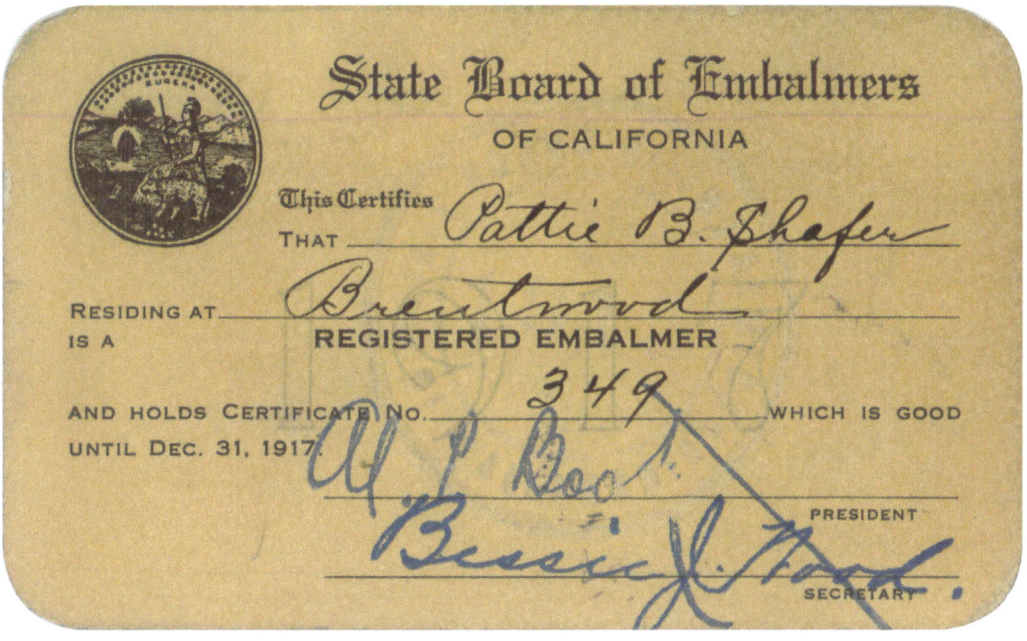

George Shafer's wife, Martha ("Patti" or "Patty") Shafer, was the first woman in California licensed as a mortician.

Dedicated to Those Who Served

VETERAN'S MEMORIAL

Community residents serving in the United States military services rest at the Union Cemetery. We honor those who have served. Each Memorial Day a United States flag is placed at each Soldier, Sailor, Marine and Coast Guard grave marker. These men and women include those serving in the following wars, police actions and conflicts.

- U.S. Civil War/War between the States (1861–1865)
- Spanish-American War (1898)
- World War I (1914–1918)
- World War II (1939–1945)
- Korean War (1950–1953)
- Vietnam War (1960–1975)
- Persian Gulf War (1990–1991)
- Invasion of Afghanistan (2001–Present)
- Invasion of Iraq (2003–2011)

CEMETERY, FRATERNAL, AND RELIGIOUS SYMBOLS AND ICONOGRAPHY

Fraternal and religious organizations played an important role in pioneer societies. Communities survived and thrived on roles and responsibilities of its members. The following are a few of the symbols you can expect to see chiseled into gravestones and monuments at Union Cemetery.

Masonic Lodge (Men)

Ancient Order of United Workmen Lodge

Eastern Star Lodge (Women)

Star of David (Religion: Judaism)

Independent Order of Odd Fellows Lodge (Men): Initials stand for Friendship, Love & Trust

Cross (Religion: Christianity)

Donner Parlor, No. 193. Native Daughters of the Golden West Byron, California

Native Sons of the Golden West

Historic Union Cemetery

HISTORIC UNION CEMETERY

Courtesy of

THE EAST CONTRA COSTA HISTORICAL SOCIETY

Begin your exploration of the pioneer graves in Union Cemetery just inside the property at the corner of Oleander Lane and Brentwood Boulevard (Highway 4). These are the oldest graves in the cemetery and rest in the original four-acre parcel sold to the cemetery district by Colburn Preston in 1878. His deed stated the land was for the purpose of establishing the Point of Timber community's first dedicated cemetery. The oldest marked grave in the cemetery is for Margaret Easton (Unit 1, Lot 39) who passed at age ten in 1865. The second oldest grave is for Gallant Lee Veale (Unit 1, Lot 45) who passed at age one or two in 1867 who is buried with her father and mother. Infant or early childhood mortality was common in pioneer America. Yes, even in eastern Contra Costa County.

Your historical walk at the Union Cemetery begins best at the oldest graves which are all located at the northwest corner of the property and are interred in four rows of underground burial units. Begin with Unit One. See the overview map of the cemetery provided on page 60. A map of each identifying unit is provided at the beginning of each section. Each unit is identified by a color.

UNIT ONE

Brentwood Boulevard

1	16	18	29	33	46
2	15	19	32	34	45
3	14	17	31	35	44
4	13	20	30	36	93

Oleander Lane — *Carriage Pathway*

Cypress Lane

UNKNOWN Unit 1, Lots 1, 2, 3, 4

Union Cemetery "Potters' Field" lies along the western most edge of Unit One. Unidentified individuals were interred with the anonymous designation "UNKNOWN." Some graves moved from the Wills ranch lost their individual identity over time.

Other graves marked only with a wooden marker deteriorated over time and the pioneer's name lost. In some instances, infant mortality resulted in the grave identification just as "Baby."

BARKLEY, Simon Taylor (1847–1941)
Unit 1, Lot 14
BARKLEY, Sarah E. (1862–1932)
Unit 1, Lot 14

Simon Barkley was born and raised in Iowa. He came to California to visit his brother, Lazarus, in 1876. Simon married Sarah Sullenger living on Deer Valley road. They met at a dinner dance at the Point of Timber Grange Hall in 1880. Judge Wallace performed their marriage ceremony, the second recorded marriage in the Brentwood Township. They settled in the Vasco region and farmed until 1908 when they moved to the property where the Brentwood Community Center is today. Their original Vasco property is now under the Los Vaqueros Reservoir. Note the symbol carved above Sarah's name. She was a member of the Eastern Star Lodge. Each of their seven boys and five girls graduated from Liberty Union High School. Five sons graduated from college, which was exceptional for the times. Simon is United States Congressman Richard Pombo's great-grandfather.

Simon Barkley (center on chair) poses with his seven sons: (left to right) James, George, Joe, Hank, Charlie, Robert and Ted.

Unit One   11

DEAN, Robert Garwood (1831–1920)
Unit 1, Lot 44
DEAN, Jerusha H. (1836–1925)
Unit 1, Lot 44

Robert Garwood Dean came to California from New York in 1850 on the schooner *Francisco*, which turned out to be a seven-month trip. He built a log cabin in Bear Valley, intending to prospect for gold, but Indians stole his mule and supplies. During the twenty years that followed, Robert worked for his uncle, Seneca, in Stockton; hunted game in the Delta; followed the gold rush to British Columbia; worked for the Hudson Bay Company; returned to California to open a store for silver prospectors; built a two-story hotel; taught school in Nevada, and managed a grocery store. Along this journey he met and married his wife Jerusha (1836–1925). She is buried with him at this site. Eventually Dean became a wheat farmer and businessman in east Contra Costa. He was the first president of the Bank of Brentwood as financially backed by Balfour Guthrie & Co. He was also instrumental in establishing a high school in Brentwood.

The Balfour Guthrie & Co. construction crew under the direction of Hercules Logan (see p. 57) poses in front of the newly built Bank of Brentwood (1913).

GLASS, John S. (1842–1904)
Unit 1, Lot 3

We know very little about John Glass except he was an early grain farmer in the Point of Timber area. He had a wife and at least one child, a son. Glass's gravestone is unique in the Union Cemetery. It incorporates the organizational symbol of the Ancient Order of United Workmen ("A.O.U.W."). This was a fraternal organization similar in its rites to the Masonic Lodge. It had lodges throughout the United States and Canada, providing mutual social and financial support after the American Civil War. It was the first of the "fraternal benefit societies" which were the first organizations to offer insurance as well as sickness, accident, death and burial policies.[7] The Point of Timber lodge was instituted on April 12, 1870 and was one of several fraternal men's organizations in the district.[8]

---

7. Schmidt, Alvin J. *Fraternal Orders* (Westport, CT: Greenwood Press), 1930, p. 82
8. Hulaniski, Frederick. *The History of Contra Costa County, California* (Published by Elms Publishing Co., Inc. Berkeley, CA) 1917, p. 425

The John Glass home, barns, outbuildings and grain fields located at Point of Timber.
Date unknown. Source: Ancestry.com accessed September 20, 2020

The Christian Heidorn Family: (Left to Right) Standing are Henry and Edna. Sitting are Christian and wife, Dorothy ("Dora" "Dorothea").

HEIDORN, Christian ("Crist") (1848–1908) Unit 1, Lot 34
HEIDORN, Dorothy ("Dora" "Dorothea") (1855–1951) Unit 1, Lot 34

Christian Heidorn came to California with brother Heinrich in 1868 from Germany, where they had been forest rangers for the government. He purchased 240 acres in the Knightsen area in 1871 and returned to Germany to claim his bride, Dorothea Steverson. By the 1890s, Heidorn Ranch had increased to more than 800 acres, dedicated to wheat, nuts, fruit and a fine vineyard. Produce was shipped to market via Babbe's Landing. He was the first president of the Knightsen Irrigation Company.

Dorothy ("Dora") Heidorn taken later in life. Dora lived to almost 100 years of age and is one of the longest lived individuals buried at the Union Cemetery.

HEIDORN, Henry W. (1875–1946) Unit 1, Lot 34

In 1904, Henry Heidorn, the son of Christian, established and ran Heidorn General Store with his sister, Emma White, nee Heidorn on Knightsen's Main Street. Henry also served the community as Justice of the Peace. He was instrumental in forming the Knightsen Irrigation Company and was Knightsen's postmaster for many years.

*H. W. Heidorn General Merchandise store circa 1920, Knightsen.
Henry Heidorn and his sister, Emma White, nee Heidorn managed the store.*

Henry W. Heidorn in retirement sitting on the porch of his Antioch home.

HILL, Edna, nee, Heidorn (1892–1975) Unit 1, Lot 34

Edna Heidorn Hill was the youngest of Christian and Dora's three children. She attended San Jose Normal College, now San Jose State University, for two years and returned in 1912 to teach at Eden Plains School. Family lore has it that as many as three teachers preceding her had been run off by some older students, teenagers and grown men who had been in the eighth grade for several years. Edna put the bullies in their place, making way for the serious students. She became the Superintendent of the Brentwood School District in 1930, an office she held for seven years before returning to the classroom. On May 15, 1955, the Brentwood Middle School was named Edna Hill School to honor Brentwood's most distinguished educator. Edna retired in 1964. She is survived by her two stepsons and hundreds of her students including the compilers of this book.

California State Flags are placed throughout the cemetery by the Native Daughters of the Golden West, Donner Parlor #193, Byron at the graves of its members. Edna Hill was a stalwart member of the organization all her life.

HILL, Sam (1876–1945) Unit 1, Lot 30

Sam Hill was originally from Downieville, California, located between Sierraville and Nevada City, where he dropped out of school at the age of ten to work for his hometown newspaper, the *Mountain Messenger*. He purchased the *Brentwood News* from Edward Kynoch in 1920 and is credited with installing electronically driven printing equipment and increasing the paper's circulation to 650. The *News* building was originally located where the Daylite Market, now Brentwood Emporium, is located. A widower with two sons, he married Edna Heidorn in 1924. Hill is buried next to his first wife, Annie Ackley Hill (1875–1922) who predeceased him by 23 years. In 1931, Sam sold the *Brentwood News* to Edgar Allen.

SANFORD, Charles E. (1851–1925)
Unit 1, Lot 30

Charles Sanford was the primary investor in the Brentwood Coal Mine also known as the Los Meganos Coal Mine operation. Mining stock speculation and considerable effort went into developing a commercial mining operation on the John Marsh land grant from 1868 to 1877. Lignite coal mining operations in Nortonville, Judsonville and Somersville fed the speculation frenzy at the newly created Pacific Stock Exchange in spite of a discouraging report from the Whitney Land Survey. Sanford subsequently filed for bankruptcy in 1875 but not before creating a Brentwood legacy. Sanford sold to the San Pablo and Tulare Railroad interests the property for a depot, acreage comprising the original Brentwood Township, and a railroad right of way through his remaining land holdings.

SANFORD, Josephine L.
(b. unknown–1897) Her will requests burial at Cypress Lawn Memorial Park, San Mateo, CA. Unconfirmed

Miss Josephine Sanford, sister of Charles Sanford, never married. This generous woman lived in Brentwood with her brother and gifted land to the community of Brentwood in 1888 with the provision it be used only as a park. Since the town was not incorporated at the time, the Contra Costa County Board of Supervisors appointed a board of three to administer what is today's Brentwood City Park. For many years, however, the property remained undeveloped. In the 1920s, it was a favorite place to escape the heat of summer under the eucalyptus trees. Originally referred to as Brentwood Grove, it is located on Second Street next to Liberty High School.

Sterling silver offering plate still used today at the Brentwood United Methodist Church.

Miss Sanford was an ardent Methodist and supporter of United Methodist Church in Brentwood. The sterling silver offering plate passed amongst the congregation on Sundays still today is her gift to the church. The engraving reads, "Bring an offering and come into his love." Next time you attend the United Methodist Church in Brentwood, take note of the offering plate and the underside engraving, "Methodist Episcopal Church, Brentwood Presented by Josephine L. Sanford June 27/94." She is gone but not forgotten.

VEALE, Richard R. (1864–1937)
Unit 1, Lot 45

Richard Rains Veale, born in Sonoma County, arrived in the Eden Plains region with his family at the age of four in 1868. He received his education at local schools (Iron House School) and began stock raising and farming on Veale Tract. He was a prominent farmer as a young man and is credited with being the first in the area to use modern methods such as the steam plow and steam harvesters. Veale attended many state conventions and served on the Republican State Committee. He became the Contra Costa County Sheriff in 1894 when the county was still untamed and served continuously until 1935. At the time, this was a record for the longest continuous service of any Sheriff in the United States. Following that, Richard was elected Treasurer of Contra Costa County, a post he held until his death in 1937.

Veale was connected with many prominent criminal cases capturing murderers, thieves, mountebanks, and recovering over $300,000 of gold bullion stolen from the Selby Smelting Company and hidden in San Francisco Bay. *[Editor's note: $300,000.00 U.S. dollars in 1901 is the equivalent of $9,328,814.00 in 2019 U.S. dollars given the U.S. Consumer Price Index. That is quite a haul!]*

Veale was also instrumental in gaining the State Highway along the San Francisco Bay, which he obtained by inducing various corporations to build the road through their property or to contribute financially to the building fund.[9] *[Editor's Note: The Bay in this instance starts in Antioch and proceeds west to the Alameda County line.]*

---

9. Hulaniski, Frederick J. *The History of Contra Costa County, California*, (Published by Elms Publishing Co., Inc. Berkeley, CA) 1917 p. 565–566

GALLAGHER, Amanda E. (1849–1880)
Unit 1, Lot 44

Henry Gallagher was an early settler and farmer in the Point of Timber district. In addition, Gallagher was the Contra Costa County Tax Collector from 1877 to 1878. Lost to history is the importance of his wife, Amanda Gallagher. Amanda holds the unique distinction of managing Mead's Hot Springs, later to be known as the world-famous Byron Hot Springs. The property owner, Louis Risdon Mead, secured inherited ownership to the 160-acre Springs property from his uncle Orange Risdon's estate in 1866. The Risdon family's initial 1861 plan was to commercially develop the salt deposits. That proved unfeasible. Orange's nephew and heir, Louis Mead saw the property's recreational and medicinal water possibilities. Unpaying Native-Americans and Yankee squatters were the problem. He erected a few structures, bathhouses, cleaned the springs and located camping areas. Importantly, Mead hired the Gallaghers as the onsite, resident managers and gatekeepers to collect hotel, cabin, camping and day use guest fees for hotel stay and enjoyment of the restorative waters. The Gallaghers lived on the property with

their three children. Amanda Gallagher died at the Springs. Her husband, Henry Gallagher, eventually left the Point of Timber area to live out the rest of his years in Colorado. Amada died prematurely at age 30 leaving her husband and children behind. She is buried here at Union Cemetery. Henry Gallagher's gravesite is unknown but presumed to be in Colorado, his final home.

Mead's Hot Springs, also known as Point of Timber Hot Springs, when under the management of Henry and Amanda Gallagher.

20 *Historic Union Cemetery*

UNIT TWO

Continue your exploration of the graves within Unit Two which is located due east of Unit One.

Brentwood Boulevard

47	60	61	76	77	92
48	59	62	75	78	91
49	58	63	74	79	90
96	57	64	73	80	89

Carriage Pathway — *Memorial Lane*

Cypress Lane

ALLEN, Edgar, Sr. (1889–1977)
Unit 2, Lot 73

ALLEN, Gertrude H. (1893–1967)
Unit 2, Lot 73

Edgar Allen came to Brentwood from the Midwest in 1931. He and his wife, Gertrude, purchased the *Brentwood News* from Sam Hill and published the weekly for more than 25 years. When he bought the paper, it was operated in a small frame building on First and Chestnut streets. In 1950, Allen built the *Brentwood News* office on Third Street. One of Allen's most popular columns in the paper was entitled, "Over the Back Fence." Allen sold the *Brentwood News* to Loyal and Janice Bisby of Oakland in 1955.

Unit Two 21

BENN, Marshall ("Marty") (1878–1984) Unit 2, Lot 73

Marshall Benn moved to Brentwood in 1893 at the age of fifteen. His grandfather, Austin Howard, had settled earlier in the Marsh Creek region. Benn was Brentwood's first superintendent of city water works and sewage treatment plant, from 1944 until his retirement in 1954. He died in 1984 at the age of 106 and is believed to be the oldest person buried in Union Cemetery. His wife, Mable (1886–1963) rests here with her husband. Marshall is the grandfather of Patrick McHenry, former owner of the Brentwood Funeral Home.

The Kelso Homestead in Point of Timber circa 1890. William Kelso stands on the far right.

KELSO, William (1842–1931) Unit 2, Lot 6
KELSO, Margaret Ann (1849–1921) Unit 2, Lot 6

William Kelso was born in Ireland and arrived in California via New York in 1870. That same year he married Margaret Armstrong and established a homestead five miles south of today's Byron. The couple had seven children, two daughters and five sons, of which four survived to adulthood. All their children have played a role in east County history in agriculture, civic involvement and peacekeeping. John ("Jack") Kelso was a prominent member of the community, Constable of Byron, and coincidentally a friend of author, Jack London, who docked at Point of Timber Landing to visit his friends and imbibe at the Byron Hot Springs. Kelso road in Byron is named after the family.

BONNICKSON, Hans (1847–1909)
Unit 2, Lot 48

Hans Bonnickson came to Brentwood in 1874, four years before the Southern Pacific Railroad arrived in east Contra Costa County. The Bonnickson family came from Denmark and settled on a parcel of land on the corner of Sellers Avenue and Chestnut Street. Hans was a wheat farmer and key player in the early development of this region. He was instrumental in establishing Liberty Union High School and was the first school board president.

The original County educational plan was to establish one high school in Antioch to accommodate students in all east Contra Costa County. Hans Bonnickson and Robert Dean traveled to Martinez and lobbied the Board of Supervisors successfully to establish a second high school for east Contra Costa County in Brentwood. That had not been the original plan at all. The Antioch/Brentwood school rivalry goes way back.

CAREY, Joseph Percy (1833–1910)
Unit 2, Lot 49

Joseph Carey, a native of Amsterdam, New York, crossed the plains at the age of twenty with brother, Levi, seeking gold. He married Mary A. Steel on November 19, 1861. Regrettably, she died of consumption (tuberculosis) after less than two years of marriage. In February 1866 he married Laura A. Welch of Illinois with whom he had five children. With the Tulare and San Pablo Railroad surveying a new route, Carey saw opportunity. One of Brentwood's first residents, Carey established the very first business in Brentwood. He and partner Solomon P. Davis established a blacksmith and repair service in 1874 with the firm name "Carey & Davis Blacksmith."[10]

---

10. Slocum, *The History of Contra Costa County* (W. A. Slocum, San Francisco., Publishers) 1881, p. 538

COPLE, George (1836–1923)
Unit 2, Lot 43
COPLE, Elsie (1877–1940)
Unit 2, Lot

George Cople traveled to New York from Switzerland when he was seventeen. Three years later, he signed on with the military and eventually traveled to Benicia where he worked for local farmers. In 1867 George purchased acreage near Point of Timber and became a successful wheat farmer. He met and wed Elsie Johnson. A scarcity of rain led him to become the first to experiment with pumping water to higher land for irrigation, opening vast new areas for farming. The test result from this irrigation "concept" doubled the alfalfa crop yield from two cuttings a year using traditional dry farming techniques to an amazing four cuttings a year thanks to the benefit of irrigation. Eureka! Thanks to his successful proof of concept, Cople convinced his farming neighbors of the value of irrigation and helped establish the Byron-Bethany Irrigation Company. He served on the first board of directors.

George and Elsie Cople pose on the front porch of their home on their wedding day.

The prosperous Cople Ranch, Point of Timber, as depicted in "Illustrations of Contra Costa County, California with Historical Sketch" as published by Smith and Elliot publishers, 1879, p. 28.

The remains of the Cople house as depicted in the above illustration in the late 20th Century.

Unit Two   25

GEYSER, Dr. Harry (1903–1973) Unit 2, Lot 89
GEYSER, Violet Woods (1907–1998), Unit 2, Lot 89

Dr. Harry Geyser and his wife, Violet, came to Brentwood in 1940 and took over the practice of Dr. E. Leavenworth. In 1942, when World War II began, Dr. Geyser volunteered for service in the U.S. Army Medical Corps and was commissioned a Captain. He left Army service with the rank of Major and returned to Brentwood to resume his medical practice. Upon his return he was appointed as high school athletic physician. Dr. Geyser served Liberty Union High School very loyally for 29 years until his retirement in 1970.

KRUMLAND, Judge Henry G.
(1880–1946) Unit 2, Lot 92

Henry Krumland was born on the family farm in Byron in 1880 and lived his entire life in east Contra Costa County. He is the son of George Krumland, a native of Germany, who came to America in 1848, and to California in 1850 via Cape Horn. The father engaged in mining for about ten years. He removed to Contra Costa County, where he found employment at ranching. Later he leased land and engaged in farming and stock raising. He died in July, 1904. The mother of Henry G. Krumland was a native of Maryland. She was the mother of ten children,

After high school, Henry enrolled in a business course and returned to Byron in 1907 to work at Lorenzo Plumley's Mercantile. In 1909, he was elected Justice of the Peace for Byron Township, an office he held for more than thirty years. The judge's office was located in the back of Plumley's store. He served the Byron community faithfully as judge, notary public, manager of the local mercantile and leader of numerous fraternal organizations. He was affiliated with the Independent Order of Odd Fellows (IOOF), Byron Lodge and was a member of the Native Sons of the Golden West, Byron Parlor #170. Henry is credited with much of Byron's early development.

NETHERTON, Edward W. (1869–1935)
Unit 2, Lot 64

Edward W. Netherton established the *Brentwood Enterprise* having bought the *Brentwood News* physical plant as established by Fred Eachus in 1897. The first newspaper established east of Antioch was the *Brentwood Courier* established in 1892 but the paper had only one issue, so it hardly counts.[11] Edward W. was the son of John Smith Netherton, a direct descendant of Capt. John Smith of Pocahontas fame, born April 30, 1835 in Clay County, Missouri.[12] The senior Netherton settled in the Point of Timber area in 1857 to farm. The younger Netherton located the newspaper office in a small cottage on Oak Street between First and Second Streets shortly after a 1910 court decision settled the Marsh Grant (Rancho los Meganos) litigation. Acquisition of the original Marsh Grant by the British owned Balfour Guthrie & Co of San Francisco, caused a boom in the district. Netherton, who had grown up in east Contra Costa County saw an opportunity to expand his burgeoning newspaper business by establishing the *Brentwood Enterprise* in Brentwood. Netherton had publishing interests elsewhere with a partner in Soquel, Santa Cruz County, beginning in 1887. Netherton established and wholly owned the *Santa Cruz Daily Evening Herald* in 1891. Netherton sold his local Brentwood paper and returned to oversee his Santa Cruz newspaper operations.[13, 14]

---

11. Monroe-Fraser, J. P. *The History of Contra Costa County,* 1926 p. 168
12. Sanford, Harrison Edward, *History of Santa Cruz County, California*, Pacific Press 1892, p. 352
13. Harrison, Edward Sanford, *History of Santa Cruz County, California*, Pacific Press 1892, p. 352
14. Portrait, Netherton, Edward W. Find a Grave. https://www.findagrave.com/memorial/8085963/edward-wallace-netherton accessed September 20, 2020

WALLACE, Judge Robert, Justice of the Peace (1859–1946) Unit 2, Lot 63

Robert Wallace was born in San Francisco. His parents moved to east Contra Costa when he was twelve, purchased 160 acres of land south of Brentwood and were among the first wheat producers in the region. Robert was elected Justice of the Peace for the Brentwood Township in 1903 and held the position for many years. His office was located in a small building that is the La Costa Taqueria today. Not only the headquarters for judicial and business affairs, it was a place to buy wood, coal and ice or bathe in the tub at the rear. His nearby home was one of the three "mansions" located on Railroad Boulevard, now Brentwood Boulevard. (See photo page 30.) At one time, Wallace was one of the largest property owners in Brentwood with seven properties located between his home and the Brentwood Park ("The Grove"). He was instrumental in establishing the Bank of Brentwood and the first to sell Home & Connecticut Hartford Insurance to residents and business owners.

Justice of the Peace, Robert Wallace standing in front of the Justice Office located where Geddes Music is located today off of Brentwood Boulevard.

The Wallace home on Railroad Avenue, now Brentwood Boulevard, Brentwood.

UNIT THREE

Continue your visit to Union Cemetery by re-crossing your steps and returning to the western edge of the cemetery.

Cypress Lane

5	12	21	28	37	94
6	11	22	27	38	43
7	10	23	26	39	42
8	9	24	25	40	41

Oleander Lane (left) — *Preston Pass* (right)

Donner Pass

ARMSTRONG, John Samuel (1843–1916), Unit 3, Lot 94

John Samuel Armstrong and his wife, Mary Ann Conner Armstrong, were both born in Ireland. They came to the Byron area in 1876, settling where the Byron Airport is today. They had seven boys and three girls. John was a "custom bailer," and hired himself out to bail hay throughout the region. In 1886, John and several of his neighbors founded the Byron Hot Springs School District on the Armstrong farm, and John served as the first school board president.

John S. Armstrong (standing far left) shown with students on the porch of the Byron Hot Springs District School house.

Unit Three   31

BUNN, William ("Billy") (1922–1988)
Unit 3, Lot 8
BUNN, Alice June (1923–Unknown)
Unit 3, Lot 8

Bill was first and foremost a farmer for the greater part of his life. He always felt a strong commitment to serve his community and was involved in many organizations and committees. He was a strong supporter of all Byron community efforts.

His greatest love and one of his finest achievements was serving on the Board of Education for Byron Union School District for 20 years from 1957–1977. Bill was intensely interested in young people and was always supportive of methods to enhance their education. He often served as president of the Board of Education. In 1977, the Byron Union School District administration building was named the William Bunn Administration Building in his honor. Bill Bunn was inducted into Liberty Union High School Athletic Hall of Fame in 1993.

Bill and June Bunn shown on their wedding day.

June Bunn taught at Knightsen School beginning in 1945 and taught classes for 37 years until retiring from the grammar school classroom in 1984

32   *Historic Union Cemetery*

DAINTY, James Ball (1837–1917)
Unit 3, Lot 10

In 1853, James and Elizabeth Dainty traveled by ship from England to Australia where they lived for several years before continuing on to California. They settled in Pittsburg where James worked for the coal mines. In 1875, they applied for and received a 160-acre land grant near the Briones Valley, but did not begin farming until the children were old enough to help with chores. In 1889, their youngest son, William, married Ella Nicholson and later purchased thirty acres of land near Brentwood so their children could attend high school. Ella lived to be 99 and is one of the oldest persons buried in the cemetery. Their daughter, Zelma Seabury, lived to be 102 years old and is buried in another section of the cemetery. Dainty's great, great grandson is the prior owner of the Brentwood Funeral Home, Patrick McHenry.

PRESTON, Colburn J. (1837–1925)
Unit 3, Lot 83
PRESTON, Marissa M. (1843–1917)
Unit 3, Lot 83

Colburn Preston arrived in California in 1868 via the Isthmus of Panama by far the fastest route from the east. Few made it to California in the promised six weeks and some not at all. Malaria, yellow fever or cholera often struck the travelers either on the jungle trip across the Isthmus or during the long wait in Panama City for the northbound ship. Colburn Preston became a successful farmer in this area and donated four acres to establish the Point of Timber Union Cemetery in 1878.

Marissa Preston (reclining far left in invalid chair). Colburn Preston (sitting far right with his grandson on his knee. Their children and grandchildren stand behind their parents.

The Preston home as it appeared in the early 20th century when the Preston family still lived there.

The Preston home as it still stands today. [Photograph thanks to Steve M. Verduzco]

WILDER, Frances E., nee Donner
(1840–1921) Unit 3, Lot 41

WILDER, William R. (1823–1886)
Unit 3, Lot 41

Frances was one of five daughters of Capt. George Donner, the leader of the ill-fated Donner Party. Frances was nearly seven in 1846 when the 29 men, 15 women, 43 children and 23 ox-drawn wagons became stranded in heavy snow in the Sierras near what is now known as Donner Lake on their trek to California. Infamous for having to resort to cannibalism, many froze or starved to death. But young Frances was rescued and taken to Sacramento. She married William R. Wilder in 1858, and they settled on a farm at Point of Timber. The Native Daughters of the Golden West, Donner Parlor #193, Byron is aptly named in her honor. Two of William and Frances' grandsons, Delmar and Donner Wilder, lived their entire lives in Byron.

William Wilder came to Point of Timber in 1865 and built a small house. He then moved his wife and family to the community from Sacramento.[15, 16]

---

15. Hulaniski, Frederick J., *History of Contra Costa County, California* (Published by Elms Publishing Co., Inc. Berkeley, CA) 1917, p. 427
16. McLaughlin, Mark, Francis E. Donner portrait, Mic Mac Publishing

Unit Three   35

WILLS, Sylvester M. (1846–1917)
Unit 3, Lot 38

WILLS, Lucretia (1848–1942)
Unit 3, Lot 38

Sylvester Wills was a wheat farmer at Point of Timber during the 1860s. His wife, Lucretia, taught at the Iron House School east of Oakley. He is credited with the early development of the Union Cemetery, shareholder in the Point of Timber Landing, creation of the Byron-Bethany Irrigation System and establishment of schools. He also donated a half-acre of land for the Grange hall, which served as the heart of the Point of Timber district. The hall served as an all-purpose community center utilized for dances, voting, receptions, community meetings, church activities and school functions. With the advent of the railroad, the community of Point of Timber became less economically important as the railroad shipping towns of Byron and Brentwood were established. Wills ranch was the informal burial place for many until the Union Cemetery was established in 1878.

```
                            Deed
    ( First deed for a burial lot made by Union Cemetery Association )

                            Deed
    Union Cemetery Association to Sylvester M. Wills, Dated Feb. 28, 1879

    Know all men by these presents, that we George Fellows, Math Berlinger, W. T.
Grover, A. Plumley, S. K. Wills, A. Richardson, D. J. Preston
Trustees of Union Cemetery Association, all of the County of Contra Costa,
State of California, in consideration of the sum of $20.00 twenty dollars to us
in hand paid by Sylvester M. Wills, the receipt whereof is hereby acknowledged,
do hereby  sell and convey unto the said Sylvester M. Wills, a certain lot
being numbered No. (38) thirty eight in the cemetery grounds deeded to said
Trustees and their successors by Colburn J. Preston and wife, deed dated
November 1st AD 1878 and recorded in the office County Recorder of Contra
Costa County aforesaid lot being numbered and described according to the
Survey and Plot of said Cemetery grounds made by R. M. Jones and filed in the
office of the Recorder of Contra Costa County October, 1878.

    To Have and to Hold the same unto the said Sylvester M. Wills, His heirs,
executors, administrators, and assigns forever, subject to all the conditions
contained in said Deed of conveyance from Colburn J. Preston and wife,
to said Trustees and their successors in office, and  subject, also to all
By-Laws, Rules and Regulations which have been or which here-after may be
passed by said Trustees or their successors.

    In Witness Whereof I, George P Fellows, President of said Board of Trustees,
in the name and in behalf of said Trustees have hereunto set my hand and seal, as the
signature and seal of said Board of Trustees, this 28th day of February AD 1879.


                                George Fellows
                                President Board of Trustees Union Cemetery
                                                              Association
```

UNIT FOUR

The last unit of the original four-acre cemetery is located east of Unit Three.

Cypress Lane

95	56	65	72	81	88
50	55	66	71	82	87
51	54	67	70	83	86
52	53	68	69	84	85

Preston Pass (left) — *Memorial Lane* (right)

Donner Pass

LeGRANDE, Alexander J. ("Tobe")
Unit 4, Lot 85. No gravestone

Tobe LeGrande was elected as Byron's constable in 1896, a position he held for more than thirty years. On December 20, 1902, one of the most disastrous train wrecks in California history occurred in Byron. The Owl Limited, bound for Los Angeles from Oakland, developed a leaking tube in the locomotive's boiler, causing escaping steam that threatened to extinguish the boiler fire. The train labored to a standstill in Byron. Meanwhile, the Stockton Flyer, a behind-schedule commuter train, was speeding down the tracks and ran into the Owl's rear coach, traveling six feet into the diner car. The impact killed 27 passengers and injured many more. Before the "wrecking train" could reach Byron, townsmen were cutting their way into the wreckage to carry out the injured. Our hero, Tobe, was seen clambering over the tangled mound of iron and steel to carry a child to safety.

On March 5, 1923, seven buildings on Byron's Main Street were destroyed by a fire that started in Manuel Rodrick's barbershop. Two young men were horsing around and accidentally knocked over a gasoline heater. Tobe happened to be entering the shop at the time and grabbed the heater, intending to throw it into the street. It exploded in his hands and engulfed him in flames. A bystander smothered the flames with his coat but not before LeGrande suffered severe burns and scarring. Seven buildings burned down, essentially all of Byron, including LeGrande's barbershop.

Unit Four 37

During the prohibition years, 1920 to 1932, Byron's three saloons stayed open as billiard halls. Rumor had it that a regular patron could purchase bootleg whiskey by the drink if the bartender knew him. Local law enforcement was aware of the illegal transactions, but looked the other way; the word was out that Constable LeGrande and Judge Krumland were two of the tavern's best customers.

McCABE, Thomas (1810–1888)
Unit 4, Lot 68

Thomas McCabe was born in Guernsey, Ohio, on May 28, 1810, and came to California in 1850, a five-month trip by wagon train to prospect for gold. In 1867, he purchased 160 acres of railroad land in Point of Timber and planted wheat. Thomas married his wife, Maria Peacock, also of Ohio, on January 13, 1831, and they had nine children. Their eldest son was Joseph P. McCabe.[17]

McCABE, Joseph P. (1839–1899)
Unit 4, Lot 68

Joseph McCabe, the eldest son of Thomas and Maria McCabe, was born in Illinois on June 15, 1839. When he was 28 or 29, the family moved to Contra Costa County Township Number Five (Point of Timber District) in 1868 and began farming. After attending Collegiate School in Napa City, Joseph also began farming in the Point of Timber District. He later enlarged his holdings to 320 acres on Marsh Creek Road about three miles from the Point of Timber post office where he served as postmaster for seven years beginning about 1872. Joseph married Miss Maggie Andrews, also a native of Illinois. They had two children, Lester Leroy and Rosie Edith.[18]

---

17. Slocum, *History of Contra Costa County* (W.A. Slocum, San Francisco., Publishers) 1881, p. 601
18. Slocum, *History of Contra Costa County* (W.A. Slocum, San Francisco., Publishers) 1881, p. 602

NUNN, Stanley (1898–1963)
Unit 4. Lot 84
NUNN, Grace (1898–1979)
Unit, 4, Lot 84

Stanley Nunn, an east Contra Costa County agricultural leader, was known for his fruit and nut orchards. President of the California Almond Growers Exchange, he was very involved in agricultural organizations both regionally and at the State level. He served on the Liberty Union High School board for many years and was a director for the Contra Costa Flood Control and Water Conservation District. Stanley's father, George, came to the Brentwood area about 1880 and

worked as a grain harvester. Stanley's children: Ron, George and Nancy still live in the community. Grace Nunn was the first woman to serve on the Brentwood Park board of directors.

PLUMLEY, Alonzo (1830–1916)
Unit 4, Lot 95

Alonzo Plumley was born in New York on August 12, 1830, and found his way to California via Canada and then to Illinois. In 1853, Alonzo and his bride, Julia E. Chilson, a native of Massachusetts, traveled west via the emigrant trail by wagon to California. They came directly to Contra Costa County, settled in the Ygnacio Valley, and in the fall of 1864 purchased a farm of 60 acres near today's Byron, where be successfully engaged in stock-railing and farming. To Alonzo and his wife, Julia, 12 children were born: Levina Elizabeth, Sarah Eleanor, Charles Eugene, Olive A., Ida E. (wife of A. F. Byer, of Byron, died December 20, 1897), Alonzo Monroe, Lorenzo Grant, Willard Olney, Emma Lydia, Edith Orela, Lillie Julia and Lulu Maud.[19] Plumley was active in laying out and grading roads in the Byron section, and did

much towards beautifying the town. He also served on the Union Cemetery Association Board and had a hand in the irrigation project that eventually led to the Byron-Bethany Irrigation Company.[20]

---

19. Hulaniski, Frederick J. *The History of Contra Costa County, California*, (Published by Elms Publishing Co., Inc. Berkeley, CA) 1917, p. 581

20. Slocum, *History of Contra Costa County*, (W.A. Slocum, San Francisco., Publishers) 1881, p. 631

Alonzo Plumley

PLUMLEY, Lorenzo Grant (1866–1939)
Unit 4, Lot 95
PLUMLEY, Mary Jane ("Jennie")
(1879–1923) Unit 4, Lot 95

Lorenzo Grant Plumley was born January 7, 1866. His father is Alonzo Plumley (see page 39) Lorenzo was educated in the public school of the Point Timber district. He moved to Mendocino County, and took up 160 acres of redwood timber, and after spending one year in that country he returned and ranched on the Marsh grant. Here he remained for five years. In 1899 he engaged in the mercantile business in Byron, which he continued. In politics he was a Republican, but never aspired to office. Fraternally, he was a member of the Independent Order of Odd Fellows (IOOF) Byron Lodge. Plumley was united in marriage to Mary Jane ("Jennie") Gann of Brentwood, born December 1, 1879. To this union there were three children: Rodney S., born October 1, 1902; Blanche Marietta, born May 16, 1908; and Lorenzo Grant, Jr. born July 30, 1911.[21]

---

21. Hulaniski, Frederick J. *The History of Contra Costa County, California*, (Published by Elms Publishing Co., Inc. Berkeley, CA) 1917, p. 581

Over the years, two fires threatened to put him out of business, but Lorenzo simply ordered new stock and reopened each time. The store stocked grocery items, sewing notions, tools, hardware and clothing. Plumley served as the Byron postmaster for many years and his mercantile served as the official Byron U.S. post office. Judge Henry Krumland, Justice of the Peace of Byron, held trials in[22] the back offices of Plumley's store. Krumland was also retained to oversee operations of the mercantile.

---

22. Leighton, Kathy, *Footsteps in the Sand*. (Sheridan Books, Inc., Ann Arbor, MI) 2001, p. 171

Lorenzo Grant Plumley

RICHARDSON, Alpheus (1830–1915)
Unit 4, Lot 57

In 1865 Alpheus Richardson traveled overland to California from Ohio, originally in search of gold, but settled in east Contra Costa to engage in "dry farming." He married Avyette Taylor, a schoolteacher and daughter of Alexander Taylor (see page 42). Alpheus was a charter member of the Grange and a founding board member for Union Cemetery in 1878. Richardson was instrumental in building Point of Timber Landing in 1883. He was also a dedicated member of the Byron Methodist Church donating a Bible for the altar of the church.[23]

---

23. Leighton, Kathy, *Footsteps in the Sand* (Sheridan Books, Inc., Ann Arbor, MI) 2001, p. 191

TAYLOR, Alexander T. (1821–1912)
Unit 4, Lot 53
TAYLOR, Louisa B. (1812–1895)
Unit 4, Lot 53

Born in Canada on September 15, 1821, Alexander Taylor was the son of a farmer. When he was 19, his father gave him two suits of clothes and one dollar with which to leave home and seek his fortune. He attended school and farmed in Canada until fire claimed his farm in 1866. In 1845 Alexander met and married, Miss Louisa Bruce of Vermont, in Canada. The couple and family moved to California via the Panama route in 1866. In 1868, they purchased 320 acres of farmland in the Point of Timber district near where Byron Highway and Highway 4 meet today at Borden Junction, irrigating his crops from Kellogg Creek. He was one of the founding seven directors of the Union Cemetery in 1878.

Taylor was involved in building the Point of Timber Landing, ushered in the railroad to the region and became one of the most prominent and well-known men in east Contra Costa County. Taylor's daughter, Beatrice Taylor Cross, was a home economics and sewing teacher at Liberty Union High School for many years.

TAYLOR, Volney (1851–1923)
Unit 4, Lot 54
TAYLOR, Agnes E. (1851–1923)
Unit 4, Lot 54

Volney was one of Alexander and Louisa Taylor's two sons and followed his father's lead in the community. He came to California with his parents when he was 15, having received a basic education in both Canada and the city of Vallejo. Volney subsequently graduaed from Pacific Business College, San Francisco, in 1872. Volney farmed with his father for many years. He married Miss Agnes Andrews, a native of Illinois, and continued the family tradition of general farming. The Taylors owned more than 800 acres of rich farmland and grew grain and alfalfa. Volney was one of the founders of the Byron Methodist Church, leading the campaign to finance the building in 1921. He was also the first president of the Byron-Bethany Irrigation Company. In 1919, Volney subdivided some of his property. These smaller parcels are on the half-mile Taylor Lane today, which lead to the Taylor Ranch.[24]

24. Slocum, *History of Contra Costa County*, (W.A. Slocum, San Francisco., Publishers) 1881, p. 680

WILKENING, Henry (1835–1883)
Unit 4, Lot 85

Henry, a native of Hanover, Germany, lived in New York before coming to California in search of gold. He purchased property in Byron during 1877, founding the town in 1878 and becoming its first official resident and postmaster. He built a home that also served

as a boarding house, a livery stable, Byron's first saloon and a hotel, which burned down in 1884. It burned again in 1917, but was never replaced. Henry married Annie Percy in 1876 and named their only son after his town. He died of pneumonia not much later.[25]

---

25. Leighton, Kathy. *Footprints in the Sand* (Sheridan Books, Inc., Ann Arbor, MI) 2001, p. 155–156

TORRE, James ("Jimmy") (1863–1915) St. Mary Cemetery, Oakland, California

Jimmy Torre (birth name, Girolamo Govanaio Torre) came to California from Genoa, Italy, in 1880 and settled in east Contra Costa County in 1887. He purchased the first bar in Brentwood originally known as Bacigalupe's Bar in 1888 and operated the saloon until his death in 1917. Torre renamed the bar "Torre's Saloon and Ice House" and began improvements. Two small buildings were constructed behind the bar: one for ice storage and the other a bathhouse. A bath was offered at 25 cents. It is unknown whether towels and soap were extra. To accommodate customers, a hitching post and a horse trough were features in front of the saloon until the 1940s. Today we drink and dine at Sweeney's just as we did at Bacigalupe's Bar and Torre's Saloon and Ice House.

SHAFER, George H. (1866–1953)
Unit 4, Lot 82
SHAFER, Martha ("Pattie" or "Patty") Candice, nee Bainbridge (1870–1958)
Unit 4, Lot 82

George Shafer was the son of William and Elizabeth Shafer and grew up in the Eden Plains area outside of Knightsen. He attended business college in Stockton and worked in the hardware and implement industry before returning to Brentwood. He purchased Moody's stable and livery business and operated it successfully for 25 years. In 1907 George Shafer converted a four-room house at 839 First Street into Shafer's Funeral Parlor. It was the very first funeral parlor in east Contra Costa County. Services were held in the living room of the family's home. Brentwood Funeral Home is still conducting business in the original location. Behind the funeral home still stands a two-story barn where Shafer operated a local livery stable. Shafer also served as the town constable and deputy coroner. In 1931, the Shafer's enlarged their house and added a large chapel.

MOODY, Percy Jones ("Jack") (1859–1942) Unit 4, Lot 70

Jack Moody, born in Maine, was the second blacksmith to establish his business in Brentwood in 1883. Blacksmithing was crucial in 19th Century America and Moody's operations expanded to include purchase of Carey's Blacksmith shop. Moody ran both the livery stable and blacksmithing forge from 1884 to 1894.

McENTYRE, Robert N. (1828–1907), Unit 3, Lot 41
McENTYRE, Sarah Louise Childers (1834–1914), Unit 3, Lot 41

Robert Newton McEntyre was born to Jostrua McEntyre and Luetita Refro on April 25, 1828 in Randolph Count, Tennessee. He headed west, stopping in Missouri. He married Sarah Louise Childers on October 25, 1849. She is said to have been 15 years of age when wed to Robert. Sarah was born in South Carolina in approximately 1834. Eight children were born to the couple. Three of them were born in Gentryville, Missouri: John Franklin, September 10, 1850, W. Jason in 1851 and Mary. These three eldest accompanied Robert and Sarah on their covered wagon journey from St. Joseph, Missouri, along the St. Joe road, then to Oregon Trail as far as Idaho and finally across Nevada on the California Trail. The family arrived in the California gold fields in August of 1856. A fourth child was born and died enroute. The family spent some time at the mines, where they found no gold. They then settled into farming near modern day Byron in the Eden Plains area. They were early wheat farmers in this area on their property located on today's Byers Road. The remaining four children were born in California: Florence, Robert, Pearl (Parilee) and Nell. Parilee Northcut, nee McEntyre is Brentwood resident, Randy Northcut's, great grandmother. *[Contributed by Robert and Sara McEntyre's great granddaughter, Elizabeth Erro Hvolboll, and great-great grandson, Eric Hvolboll]*

Sarah Louise Childers and Robert M. McEntyre

Robert and Sarah McEntyre on their 50th wedding anniversary in 1899.

NOTABLE AND NEWER UNITS

Sections A, B, C, D, E & F

Outside the original four units at Union Cemetery are notable community members too numerous to list. They include local businesspeople, Civil War veterans, educators, mayors, newspaper editors and community leaders. Refer to the large cemetery map on page 60. Most of these individual grave markers are found in Sections B and D. The following individuals are of note.

SECTION A

SANCHEZ, Jose (1875–1946), Section A

SANCHEZ, Clotilde (1880–1950), Section A

Jose and Clotilde Sanchez, both from Andalusia, Spain, are examples of European emigrants finding opportunity in east Contra Costa County. The couple initially contracted in 1913 with the C&H Sugar Company as laborers in the Hawaiian sugar cane fields. After fulfilment of their contract, the

Sanchez's came to California in 1917 where they once again worked as contract laborers on Bradford Island. Industry, money saving habits, and availability of land in Brentwood enabled them to buy 22 acres of Brentwood Irrigated Farms (Balfour Guthrie & Co.) land. They had 11 children. Ten survived to adulthood many descendants of whom are still living in Brentwood.

SECTION B

KNIGHT, George W. (1843–1931)
Section B, Lot 14, Row 4

KNIGHT, Christina Christensen (1856–1936) Section B, Lot 14, Row 4

The founder of Knightsen was born in Maine and sailed to California in 1874 via the Isthmus of Panama. He purchased 110 acres in the Eden Plain district, which was located where the town of Knightsen is today. His wheat and hay farms were so successful, he was able to purchase the adjoining 80 acres and expand his crops to include almonds. When the Santa Fe Railroad Company wanted to route a line from Oakland to Stockton through his fields, he offered them enough land for a passing track and a station if they would move farther west and cut off just a corner of his ranch. In gratitude, the Superintendent of the Santa Fe Railroad named the town Knightsen by adding the "sen" from his wife, Christina's, maiden name, Christensen.

Notable and Newer Units

HAMMOND, Dr. James
(1856–1955) Section B

Dr. Hammond, a surprisingly diminutive man, arrived in Byron in 1898. He was 4 feet 11 inches tall and never weighed over 125 pounds. That weight excluded the pistol he always carried in his pocket. Hammond delivered hundreds of babies in east Contra Costa including his own children, grandchildren, and one great grandson when he was 89 years old. By the 1920s, Dr. Hammond maintained professional offices in Oakley, Brentwood and Byron. He could be seen often in his carriage loaded

with medical supplies making house calls. He died at the age of 99 in 1955.[26]

26. Leighton, Kathy, *Footprints in the Sand,* (Sheridan Books, Inc., Ann Arbor, MI) 2001, p. 43–44

WEEKS, Charles ("Charlie"), Sr.
(1884–1980) Section B, Lot 38

Charlie Weeks, was the first non-Scotsman appointed to manage the Balfour Guthrie & Co operations, Brentwood Irrigated Farms. He held that position from 1929 to 1970 when he retired. The Balfour & Guthrie & Co organization transformed the east Contra Costa area from dry farming of wheat and grain to the irrigated farming upon purchase of 12,500 acres of John Marsh's Rancho los Meganos in 1910. The land was transformed with the creation of irrigation systems.

Weeks was integral to the building of the Brentwood community, innovative farming techniques and ensuring the profitability of Brentwood Irrigated Farms for its parent company. There was not a fraternal or civic organization to which Weeks was not a member including: the Masonic Lodge, Lions Club, Brentwood Union High School District and Brentwood Fire Commission to name only a few. He has the distinction of being the very first City of Brentwood Citizen of the Year. Gratefully, Weeks was also an avid amateur photographer. His photographs capturing agricultural and

stock operations in the Brentwood area capture over 40 years of community evolution, farming innovation, introduction of airplanes, and irrigation methods. The fruits of much of Weeks' photography can be found at the East Contra Costa Historical Society research room.

OHMSTEDE, Theodore ("Teddy") (1907–1968) Section B, Row 3

Teddy Ohmstede moved to Knightsen with his parents at the age of three and attended primary grades in Knightsen. He graduated from Liberty Union High School in 1927. Ohmstede's Store was known for drinks, sandwiches, tobacco and hospitality. The community elected him Justice of the Peace in 1951. A bachelor all his, life, Ted was well known for his work with local youth and sports activities. The sports fields at Liberty Union High School were named in his honor in 1965 in recognition of his dedication.

The 1949 Liberty Union High School *Liberty '49er Lion* annual was dedicated to Teddy Ohmstede. He was lauded as "the one man we could count on for support and his presence at the high school sporting events, dances, etc., is as welcome as his big, friendly smile. Teddy's contributions this year are typical. During football season he was almost a daily visitor to the practice field and his strong encouragement was no small factor in landing the league championship. Teddy also bought the Varsity 22 new pairs of pants. He did it quietly, without fuss, and more important, he did it voluntarily because that's the kind of a guy he is. Above we have listed just one of his memorable deeds. But for every one we could mention, there are literally dozens to which he has contributed quietly and continuously and from which some student or the whole school has benefitted."[27]

---

27. "Our Teddy" Liberty Union High School 1949 annual, p. 2

DAVIS, O. R. ("CAL") (1884–1975),
Section B

DAVIS, Ruth T. (1891–1974),
Section B

CAL and Ruth Davis are a California success story right out of the 1930s depression. More than 80 years ago, people driven west by the Great Depression and the Dustbowl began to settle in Brentwood, setting up camps wherever they found stable ground. O. R. Davis was one of them, arriving with his wife Ruth and establishing what would become known as Davis Camp near a dumpsite at what is now the corner of Brentwood Boulevard and Sunset Road. The land the Davis' squatted on was actually owned by the county, but according to local historian Kathy Leighton, the county sold the land to Davis for a minimal fee in exchange for his pledge to keep the area clean. Davis used materials from the dump such as wood and cardboard to create temporary shelters.

During the height of the Great Depression in the early 1930s, thousands of people began to move west to escape the poverty of the Dustbowl. People often asked to stay on Davis' property, and he'd let families stay as long as they needed to. Some families paid rent, but Davis didn't pressure those who couldn't afford it.

People came and went with the changing of the seasons, but many made Davis Camp their permanent California residence. By 1934, nearly 1,000 people resided at Davis Camp. The huge population forced Davis to quit his work in the fields. He built a shed to store food and supplies for the families to share, and eventually the shed became the Davis Log Cabin Grocery, which became Los Mexicanos Market (now closed).

Despite running the market, Davis wasn't a wealthy man. He invested all his earnings to build more shelters and gather supplies to help the families living on his property. "CAL Davis didn't do it for the money," Leighton said. "He did it out of the goodness of his heart. He left a wonderful legacy of generosity. Of all the people I've interviewed about Davis Camp, I haven't heard a bad thing about him. Everyone speaks so highly of him. He left footprints on the hearts of all those families he helped."[28]

---

28. Samie Hartley, The Brentwood Press, *The Lost History of Davis Camp*. www.thepress.net Apr 30, 2009. Updated Dec 12, 2019 accessed Sep 20, 2020.

SECTION B

**FARRAR, John Junius ("Frank")
(1877–1947) Section B, Lot 10, Row 3
FARRAR, Myra Blanche, nee Frantz
(b. unknown – d. unknown)
Gravesite unknown**

Frank Farrar was born in Arkansas and was one of 12 children. He had lived in California for over 50 years, 21 years of that in the Brentwood, Oakley and Bethel Island area. Farrar is generally credited with creating, developing and marketing the recreational potential of this San Joaquin River Delta area. Bethel Island became a mecca for recreation, fishing and hunting in 1943 with the arrival of Blanche and Frank Farrar. They spotted a grove of eucalyptus trees on a parcel of land along Dutch Slough and purchased it from Judge Bridgeford. They founded Farrar Park with swimming, picnicking, and other outdoor activities. Farrar was perhaps the mainstay of Bethel Island development and was responsible for the sub-division of lots sold to recreation-minded buyers. Lots originally sold for $50.00 and little notice was given to securing a county building permit. There were more than 250 residential lots sold in Farrar Park.

Blanche Farrar was an equal partner in Frank's park, tent cabin rentals, store and development plans. Frank sold and leveraged property sales to get ahead. Frank and Blanche sold Farrar Park and bought the whole town of Cal-Pine when the lumber company moved out. They kept the president's house and sold the rest of the company

Boat Harbor, Farrar Park

town for summer homes. The process was repeated at Lake Almanor for another profit. Blanche remarried and lived in Brentwood before moving to Pollack Pines, El Dorado County. She passed at age 93. The couple is survived by a son, Frank Farrar, Jr.[29]

---

29. Gromm, Robert ("Bob") D. *Historically Speaking on the Bethel Island Area: Stories and Pictures of Years Gone By.* Self-published, Black Diamond Print & Copy, p. 189–193

NAIL, James Alliance (1892–1984)
Section B, block 28, grave 8
NAIL, Zelma (1891–1952)
Section B, block 28, grave 8

James and Zelma Nail are the Knightsen pioneers whose heirs bequeathed their home to the East Contra Costa Historical Society. The house, outbuildings, lawns and property are now the Society's home and museum. Their house was built in 1878 by an early Eden Plains pioneer, Johnson Fletcher, for his family and was used in later years as a boarding house for land speculators and travelers. It was sold to John Richard Byer and his family in 1883. He bequeathed it to his daughter, Georgia Ann.

In 1922, the house was sold to James and Zelma Sedge Nail. Upon their deaths, it became the property of their only son, Clelland. In 1986, Clelland and his wife, Marge, donated the house and one acre of land to the East Contra Costa Historical Society.

PEREIRA, Henry Stanley (1922–1986)
Section B, Grave 10, Lane F

Stanley Pereira held almost every civic position in Byron and was generally lauded as the "Mayor of Byron." A Byron native, Stanley graduated from Liberty Union High School in 1940. He served as county Deputy Marshal, Justice of the Peace, county supervisor, and his most rewarding appointment, Santa Claus to hundreds of Byron schoolchildren every year. Pereira at age 29 was the youngest judge in California at the time of his appointment in 1951 to the Byron Municipal Justice Court. He served until the Byron Court was consolidated with the Brentwood Municipal Justice Court in 1964. Pereira was not an attorney and dispensed justice as he saw fit in accordance with the law. His court was located in a building next door to the Wild Idol Saloon on Main Street, Byron. Pereira might tend bar one moment at the

Stanley Pereira at age 29 was the youngest appointed as judge in California in 1951.

Wild Idol and then remove next door to address the court case calendar docket. With justice dispensed, it was back to work behind the bar. He was a leader in the community for over 45 years.

Notable and Newer Units

BRISTOW, William ("Bill") Bryan
(1935–2009) Section D, Block 38, Lot 4

Bill Bristow, born in Arkansas, arrived in eastern Contra Costa County during the depression as a one-year-old child. He, seven siblings and his parents first lived in Geyserville where his parents worked in the vineyards. The family moved to Brentwood when Bill was in grammar school and worked on Tony Ghiozzi's farm on Marsh Creek Road. The indigent farm labor life found the family in and out of east Contra Costa County as his parents followed seasonal crop work. Eventually, Brentwood became home and Bill graduated from Liberty Union High school excelling in sports. His early desire to become an educator led Bill to San Francisco State University where he graduated in Education with a minor in history. Knightsen Elementary School provided Bill with this his first teaching job in an eighth grade classroom at age 21 and his first administrative position five years later. Administrative advancement came rapidly after that as Bill wrote curriculum and educational modules for Byron, Knightsen, Brentwood and Liberty school districts. Appointment as principal of Edna Hill School followed and subsequent employment as school district superintendent.

Bill held the position of Brentwood Superintendent of Schools for over 25 years. The William B. Bristow Middle School in Brentwood is named after him.[30]

---

30. Bristow, Bill. *I'm Bill Bristow: Where Have You Been, Billy Boy?* Park Place Publications, Pacific Grove 2009

WITH US IN SPIRIT

MARSH, John (1799–1856) with wife, Abigail ("Abbie") Smith Tuck (1818–1855), Mt. View Cemetery, Oakland

CAMERON, Alice Francis, nee Marsh (1852–1927), daughter of John and Abigail Marsh, Mt. View Cemetery, Oakland

MARSH, Charles (1826–1901), son of John and Margarete Marsh, Mt. View Cemetery, Oakland

The arrival of John Marsh, western pioneer and the first non-Hispanic settler in the interior of California, begins our local non-indigenous history.

John Marsh and his family are not buried at the Union Cemetery. John and Abby are buried at Mountain View Cemetery, Oakland. However we honor John, Abby, Charles and Alice here as this cemetery is land once part of Marsh's 14,000 to 17,000-acre Rancho los Meganos. Here is where it all began. And thanks to this tribe of Bay Miwok Native Americans, Marsh was able to make his Rancho a success.

The early years at the Marsh Grant established the crops and population that would define the State of California. Marsh introduced wheat, viticulture, orchards, dairy and cattle ranching to the Central Valley. His letters and efforts encouraging emigration from the United States to Alta California resulted in the first overland party of settlers, the Bartleson-Bidwell party, arriving in California at Marsh's Rancho in 1841. Marsh worked tirelessly behind the scenes for a peaceful transition of Mexican California into the United States. The Mexican-American War, gold discovery, and the Treaty of Guadalupe-Hidalgo would change California's political climate and Marsh's personal fortune, culminating in his murder in 1856.[31]

Marsh's wife, Abigail ("Abby" or 'Abbie') Smith Tuck Marsh perished in 1855. She was a schoolteacher from New England and principal of a school in San Jose. She had married John in 1851 and bore him one child, a daughter Alice Francis, a year later.

Charles Marsh of Prairie du Chien, Wisconsin was the son of John Marsh and his first wife, Marguerite, nee Deconteaux, and joined his father in California. Charles had been left as an infant with the Panitier family in New Salem, Illinois where he was raised. Marsh subsequently married one of his adoptive sisters, Susan Marsh, nee Panitier with whom he had seven children. His wife and all the children joined him at the Marsh Rancho once he was established in California.

John Marsh was killed by bandits in Pacheco in 1856 leaving his son, Charles Marsh and three-year old daughter, Alice Marsh, as heirs to the estate. Charles tracked down his father's murderers and

---

31. Jensen, Carol. *Images of America: Brentwood*, 2008, pp. 13–20

brought them to justice. He also served as an Antioch Justice of the Peace and Central Pacific Railroad board member.

Alice Marsh was raised by various families in the east Contra Costa Area and grew up well educated and wealthy. At age 19, Alice married Deputy Sheriff William Walker Cameron in 1871. Cameron was a politically active and influential Californian. However, Alice's money, real estate and investments disappeared under Cameron's management and bad luck. They divorced in 1891. Today we see Alice's legacy in the naming of the town of Orinda and by her home, the Cameron House, one of the last Victorian mansions preserved along Lake Merit, Oakland.

CAKEBREAD, Robert (1838–1911) Oak View Memorial Park, Antioch, California
CAKEBREAD, Martha (1840–1914) Oak View Memorial Park, Antioch, California

Robert Cakebread arrived in San Francisco in 1857 with his 17-year old bride, Martha, from Bloxham, Oxfordshire, England, via Cape Horn. After nine unsuccessful years in the Tuolumne gold fields, the Cakebread's moved to Somersville where Robert worked in the coal mines. In 1874, he purchased land in Judsonville and raised sheep. In 1879, he purchased tree-filled acreage near Marsh Creek and entered the fuel wood business, later planting wheat and grain. Robert and Martha had 15 children of which only eight survived to adulthood. According to the Cakebread family, their ancestor was a baker for the King of England, where it was common for tradesmen to take a name that reflected their craft. Therefore, a blacksmith became "Smith," and a barrel maker became "Cooper." Instead of taking the name "Baker" however, he chose to be known by what he baked, cake and bread.[32]

---

32. Leighton, Kathy, *Footprints in the Sand*, (Sheridan Books, Inc., Ann Arbor, MI) 2001, pp. 98–99

56   *Historic Union Cemetery*

FELLOWS, George (1826–1900)
Tolocay Cemetery Napa, Napa County.
FELLOWS, Ann M. (1837–1901)
Tolocay Cemetery, Napa, Napa County

George Fellows, born in New Hampshire, arrived in California after a 90-day drive from Missouri in 1850 just in time for California to become a state. He followed gold mining until 1862 when he settled in Napa. The quicksilver mining opportunities brought him to Contra Costa County where he toiled for over five years until the quicksilver vapors nearly ended his life. At that time he retired to his 320-acre, Point of Timber farm, named "Lea-Ridge." Fellows was a prominent, active citizen in Contra Costa County participating in local governance and many civic improvement projects. His submission of cinnabar ore to the 1876 Philadelphia International Exhibition earned him a medal and diploma—the only such premium awarded to Contra Costa County.[33] He was the founding president of the Union Cemetery in 1878.[34]

---

33. Smith and Elliot, *Illustrations of Contra Costa County with Historical Sketch*, 1879, p. 29
34. Smith and Elliot, *Illustrations of Contra Costa County with Historical Sketch*, 1879, p. 26

LOGAN, Hercules ("Herc") (1878–1973)
Memory Gardens, Concord, California.
LOGAN, Ethel J. (1877–1954)
Memory Gardens, Concord, California.

Hercules and Ethel Logan gravesite, Memory Gardens, Concord.

Born in Scotland, Hercules Logan was 28 when he arrived in New York. A skilled carpenter, he visited his brother in Humboldt County in 1904 and stayed to help build the Eureka City Hall. In 1912 Hercules was hired by Balfour, Guthrie & Company to build the Brentwood Hotel and the Bank of Brentwood. He settled in Brentwood and became a full-service contractor. When building a home, he would draw up the plans, furnish the materials and personally finance the entire transaction. Logan formed the foundation of Brentwood's early businesses. One could say that Logan literally built downtown Brentwood.

HAMMOND, Harry T. (1863–1941)
Gravesite location unknown

Harry Hammond, native of Napa and younger brother of Dr. James Hammond, was the publisher and editor of the *Byron Times* newspaper. Hammond started in the newspaper business at William Randolph Hearst's *San Francisco Examiner* as a cub reporter. The 1906 San Francisco earthquake and fire combined with perceived greater journalistic advancement brought him to Byron. There he founded *The Byron Times*, "The Monarch of the Weeklies" to paraphrase William Randolph Hearst's *The San Francisco Examiner*, masthead motto, "The Monarch of the Dailies." The *Byron Times* had circulation in Alameda, Contra Costa and San Joaquin Counties. It was the first newspaper in California to use red ink.[35] He was appointed California State Printer in 1931 during the Governor James ("Sunny Jim") Rolph Jr. administration and served in that post for many years. [*Editor's note: Hammond and Rolph met at the Byron Hot Springs. Rolph was a Director of the Byron Hot Springs Corporation.*] Hammond was a Byron booster to rival Sinclair Lewis' fictional character "Babbitt."

35. Hulaniski, Frederick J. *The History of Contra Costa County, California* (Published by Elms Publishing Co., Inc. Berkeley, CA) 1917, p. 428

THE BYRON TIMES

SELLERS, Samuel (1811–1888)
Mt. View Cemetery, Oakland
SELLERS, Sarah, nee Abbot (1832–1883)
Mt. View Cemetery, Oakland

Edith Sellers, daughter of Samuel and Sarah Sellers. Image dated circa 1906.

The Sellers family, like many of the pioneer families in the area, farmed the rich soil, planting wheat along with pears, peaches, olives, figs, almonds and apricots. But they also contributed in many other ways to the development of the area. Sarah Sellers formed the Iron House School District in 1861 and became the first woman school trustee in the State of California. She also planted 3,000 mulberry trees to start a silkworm farm and was highly regarded as an authority on silk cultivation. You can still see many of these original mulberry trees on Sellers Avenue and the Sellers' original home is still there. Their son, George, owned one of the finest orchards in this region growing primarily walnuts and apricots. He was a member of the Prune and Apricot Association of California where he represented the interests of the farmers. He served as a Deputy Sheriff with Sheriff Veale. Samuel and Sarah's daughter, Edith, was the first graduate of Liberty Union High School and graduated number one academically in her class of one student in 1906. Sellers Avenue, running from Dutch Slough at the north end to Highway 4 at the south end, is named in recognition of this pioneer family.

MEAD, Lewis Risdon (1847–1918)
Mt. View Cemetery, Oakland
REID, Mae Sadler Mead (1887–1965)
Olivet Memorial Park, Colma

Among the many brilliant, able and resourceful men who gained positions of distinction in the Bay cities was Lewis Risdon Mead. Mr. Mead was one of Contra Costa County's most progressive and successful businessmen, and his name had been known and honored here for many years. Lewis Risdon Mead was born in Saline, Michigan, and came to California via the Isthmus route in 1863. He joined with his uncle, John Risdon, and served as secretary and auditor of the Risdon Iron Works until 1907. Risdon secured the Springs property in 1885, improved it and opened Mead's Hot Springs under the management of H. C. and Amanda Gallagher (see page 20).[36]

Upon Mead's passing in 1918, his second wife, Mae Sadler Mead assumed ownership and management of the Springs. A darling of the San Francisco social set, Mae leased the Springs to restauranteur John Tait. It soon became a retreat for Bay Area and Southern California socialites, politicians, and the well-heeled. Mae subsequently married in 1922 one of Mead's best friends, architect James Reid. The Byron Hot Springs became a memorial to Lewis Mead's memory.

Byron Hot Springs is sometimes called the "Carlsbad of the West," after the famed European health spas. The resort hosted the famous, the wealthy, the infirm and the curious alike during the late 19th and early 20th centuries. The 160-acre property in Byron featured three grand hotels designed by renowned San Francisco architect James Reid. Amidst this stylish backdrop were prominent guests in 19th-century finery, early Hollywood royalty, Prohibition entertainments, mineral water "cures" for various ailments, and secret interrogations of World War II POWs (when it was known as "Camp Tracy"). Aside from the hot springs themselves, the resort once claimed one of the oldest golf courses in the western United States.

Louis Risdon Mead, Secretary of the Risdon Iron Works, San Francisco and proprietor of the Byron Hot Springs.

Mae Sadler Mead Reid, President of the Byron Hot Springs Corporation from 1918 to 1965. Contra Costa County Chairwoman to the 1915 Panama Pacific International Exposition. Woman's Board

The third Byron Hot Springs Hotel built in 1915 for Panama Pacific International Exposition guests still exists at the Springs. However, it is in a sad state of disrepair due to vandalism.

---
36. Hulaniski, Frederick J. *The History of Contra Costa County, California* (Published by Elms Publishing Co., Inc. Berkeley, CA) 1917, p. 161

UNION CEMETERY

Pioneer Units located at top left

Units 1 (Blue), 2 (Red), 3 (Green), & 4 (Orange)

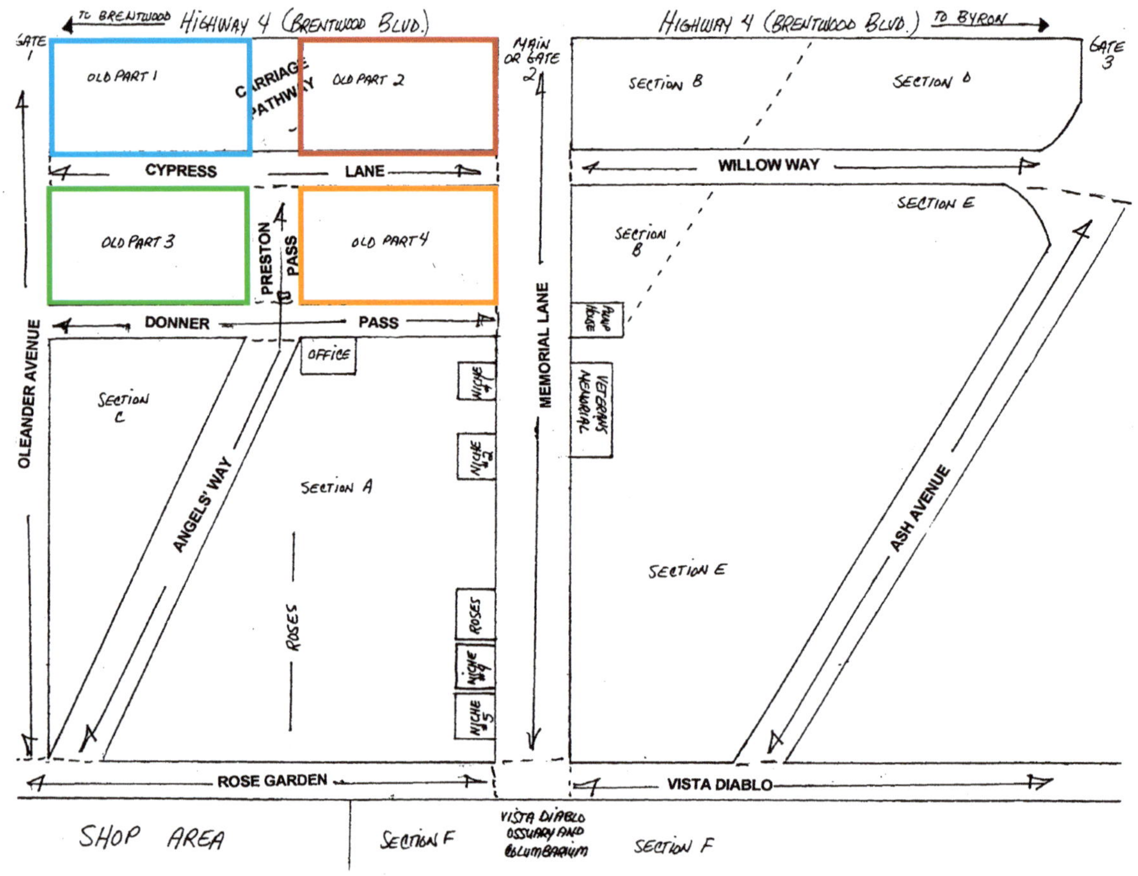

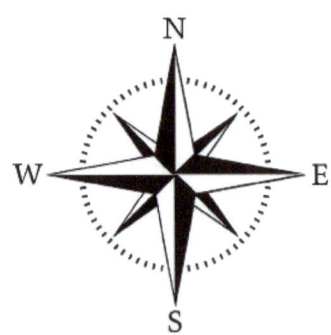

DETAILED PIONEER UNIT AREA

Old Units 1, 2, 3 & 4

HIGHWAY 4 BRENTWOOD BLVD.

UNIT ONE

1	16	18	29	33	46
2	15	19	32	34	45
3	14	17	31	35	44
4	13	20	30	36	93

UNIT TWO

47	60	61	76	77	92
48	59	62	75	78	91
49	58	63	74	79	90
96	57	64	73	80	89

Oleander Lane

CYPRESS LANE

Memorial Lane

UNIT THREE

5	12	21	28	37	94
6	11	22	27	38	43
7	10	23	26	39	42
8	9	24	25	40	41

UNIT FOUR

95	56	65	72	81	88
SO	55	66	71	82	87
51	54	67	70	83	86
52	53	68	69	84	85

Preston Pass

----DONNER PASS----

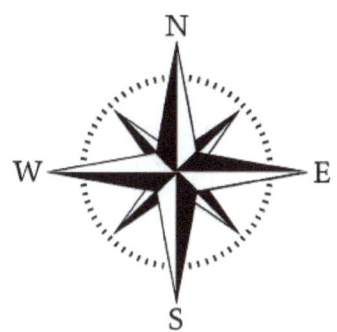

ALPHABETICAL INDEX BY FAMILY NAME

Allen, Edgar, Sr., 21
Allen, Gertrude H., 21

Armstrong, John Samuel, 31

Barkley, Sarah E., 11
Barkley, Simon Taylor, 11
Benn, Marshall ("Marty"), 22
Bonnickson, Hans, 23
Brentwood Funeral Home, 6–7
Bristow, William ("Bill") Bryan, 54
Bunn, Alice June, 32
Bunn, William ("Billy"), 32
Byron Hot Springs, 20, 59

Cakebread, Martha, 56
Cakebread, Robert, 56
Cameron, Alice, nee Marsh, 55–56
Carey, Joseph Percy, 23
Cople, Elsie, 24
Cople, George, 24

Dainty, James Ball, 33
Davis, O. R. ("CAL"), 50
Davis, Ruth T., 50
Dean, Jerusha H., 12
Dean, Robert Garwood, 12
Donner, Frances E. *See* Wilder, Frances E.
Farrar, John Junius ("Frank"), 51
Farrar, Myra Blanche, nee Frantz, 51
Fellows, Ann M., 57
Fellows, George, 57

Gallagher, Amanda E., 20
Gallagher, Henry, 20
Geyser, Dr. Harry, 26
Geyser, Violet Woods, 26
Glass, John S., 13

Hammond, Dr. James, 48

Hammond, Harry T., 58
Heidorn, Christian ("Crist"), 14
Heidorn, Dorothy ("Dora"), 14
Heidorn, Henry W., 14–15
Hill, Edna, nee Heidorn, 16
Hill, Sam, 17

Kelso, Margaret Ann, 22
Kelso, William, 22
Knight, Christina, nee Christensen, 47
Knight, George W., 47
Krumland, Judge Henry G., 27

LeGrande, Alexander J. ("Tobe"), 37–38
Logan, Ethel J., 57

Marsh, Abigail ("Abby" or "Abbie") Smith Tuck, 55
Marsh, Alice. *See* Cameron, Alice
Marsh, Charles, 55–56
Marsh, John, 55
McCabe, Joseph P., 38
McCabe, Thomas, 38
McEntyre, Robert N., 45
McEntyre, Sarah Louise, nee Childers, 45
Mead, Louis Risdon, 59
Mead's (Byron) Hot Springs, 20, 59
Moody, Percy Jones ("Jack"), 44

Nail, James Alliance, 52
Nail, Zelma, 52
Netherton, Edward W., 28
Nunn, Grace, 39
Nunn, Stanley, 39

Ohmstede, Theodore ("Teddy"), 49

Pereira, Henry Stanley, 53

Plumley, Alonzo, 30
Plumley, Mary Jane ("Jennie"), 40
Plumley, Lorenzo Grant, 40
Point of Timber, 3–4, 36
Preston, Colburn J., 33
Preston, Marissa M., 33

Reid, Mae Sadler Mead, 59
Richardson, Alpheus, 41

Sanchez, Clotilde, 46
Sanchez, Jose, 46
Sanford, Charles E., 18
Sanford, Josephine L., 18
Sellers, Samuel, 58
Sellers, Sarah, nee Abbot, 58
Shafer, George H., 44
Shafer, Martha ("Pattie" or "Patty") Candice, nee Bainbridge, 44

Taylor, Agnes E., 42
Taylor, Alexander T., 42
Taylor, Louisa B., 42
Taylor, Volney, 42
Torre, James ("Jimmy"), 43

Union Cemetery, 3–5, 10, 60
Unknown Graves ("Potter's Field"), 10–11

Veale, Richard R., 19
Veteran's Memorial, 8

Wallace, Judge Robert, 29
Weeks, Charles ("Charlie"), Sr., 48
White, Emma, nee Heidorn, 14–15
Wilder, Frances E., nee Donner, 35
Wilder, William R., 35
Wilkening, Henry, 43
Wills, Lucretia J., 36
Wills, Sylvester M., 36

SELECTED READINGS

Bristow, Bill with Don Huntington. *I'm Bill Bristow: Where Have You Been Billy Boy?* Pacific Grove: Park Place Publications, 2009.

Bohakel, Charles A. *The Indians of Contra Costa County: The Costanoan and Yokuts Indians.* Amarillo: P & H Publishers, 1977.

Bolton, Herbert E., Ed. *Fray Juan Crespi: Missionary Explorer on the Pacific Coast, 1769-1774.* Berkeley: University of California Press, 1927.

DeMartini, Carolyn. *The Brentwood Hospital: A Rural California Hospital and its Environs 1929-1931.* Concord, CA: Concord Graphics Arts, 1999.

Emanuels, George. *California's Contra Costa County: An Illustrated History.* Fresno, CA: Panorama West Books, 1986.

Emerson, Kathy. *Iron House School.* Lodi, CA: Abrahamson Printing, 1984.

Historic Record Co. *History of Contra Costa County, California, with Biographical Sketches.* Los Angeles, CA: Historic Record Co., 1926.

Hohlmayer, Earl. *Looking Back II Tales of Old East Contra Costa County: An Illustrated History.* Antioch, CA: E & N Hohlmayer, 1996

Hulaniski, Frederic J., editor. *The History of Contra Costa County, California,* Berkeley, CA: The Elms Publishing Co., 1917.

Jensen, Carol A. and the East Contra Costa Historical Society, *Images of America: Brentwood,* Mt. Pleasant, SC, Arcadia Publishing Company, 2008.

Jensen, Carol A. and the East Contra Costa Historical Society, *Images of America: Byron Hot Springs,* Mt. Pleasant, SC: Arcadia Publishing Company, 2006.

Jensen, Carol A. and the East Contra Costa Historical Society, *Postcard History East Contra Costa County,* Mt. Pleasant, SC, Arcadia Publishing Company, 2007.

Leighton, Kathy, *Footprints in the Sand.* The City of Brentwood and East Contra Costa Historical Society Publication. Ann Arbor, MI: Sheridan Books, Inc. 2001.

Lyman, George D. *John Marsh Pioneer, the Story of a Trail Blazer on Six Frontiers,* The Chautauqua Press, Chautauqua, New York, 1931, 394 pages, 24 illustrations.

Munro-Fraser, J. P. *History of Contra Costa County, California.* San Francisco, CA.

W. A. Slocum and Co., 1882 (reprint, Oakland, CA: Brooks-Sterling Co., 1974).

Noble, Vernon C. *Liberty Union High School: A Memoir*, East Contra Costa County Historical Society Brentwood. Printed and bound by Sheridan Books, Ann Arbor, MI, 2001.

Purcell, Mae Fisher. *History of Contra Costa County.* Berkeley, CA: The Gillick Press, 1940.

Sheldon, William Frederick. *Baling Dust.* Walnut Grove, CA: Camp House Press, 1984.

Smith and Elliott, *Illustrations of Contra Costa County.* Oakland, CA: Smith and Elliott, 1878 (reprint, Sacramento, CA: Sacramento Lithograph Co., 1952).

Tatam, Robert Daras, *Old Times in Contra Costa.* Pittsburg, CA: Highland Publishers, 1993.

University of California Publications in American Archaeology and Ethnology, Vol. 23, No. 2. Berkeley: University of California Press, 1926.

OTHER RESOURCES

Bay Area Office of the California Department of Water Resources. http://baydeltaoffice.water.ca.gov/

Contra Costa County Historic Landmarks Advisory Committee
http://www.co.contra-costa.ca.us/depart/cd/administration/hlac.htm

Contra Costa County Historical Society
610 Main Street
Martinez, CA 94553
http://www.cocohistory.com

Delta Wetlands Project
http://www.deltawetlands.com, 2007

East Contra Costa Historical Society & Museum
3890 Sellers Avenue
Brentwood, CA 94513,
http://www.theschoolbell.com/history

The John Marsh Historic Trust, Inc.
Dedicated to saving the historic stone house.
http://www.JohnMarshHouse.com

ABOUT THE EAST CONTRA COSTA HISTORICAL SOCIETY & MUSEUM

The purpose of the East Contra Costa Historical Society (ECCHS) is to bring together those people interested in history, and especially in the history of east Contra Costa County. Understanding the history of our community is basic to our democratic way of life; it gives us a better understanding of our state and nation, and promotes a better appreciation of our American heritage.

ECCHS's major function is discovery and collection of materials which may help to establish, illustrate and perpetuate the history of east Contra Costa County. ECCHS provides for the preservation of such materials and for their accessibility as far as may be feasible, to all who wish to examine and study them. ECCHS cooperates with officials to ensure the preservation and accessibility of the records and archives of the County and of its cities, towns, villages and institutions. ECCHS also undertakes the preservation of historic buildings, monuments and markers.

ECCHS is organized exclusively for charitable and educational purposes and qualifies as an organization under Section 501(c)3 of the Internal Revenue Code (or corresponding provisions of a future U.S. Internal Revenue law). Membership and volunteer opportunities are available to all. Individual annual dues are $20.00 and family dues are $25.00. Donations of items of local historical interest are welcome and encouraged! Your monetary donation of any amount is gratefully acknowledged and is tax-deductible to the extent allowed by law.

East Contra Costa Historical Society & Museum
3890 Sellers Avenue
P.O. Box 202
Brentwood, CA 94513
Phone Number: (925) 634-0917
Website: https://eastcontracostahistory.org
Email: ecchs@eastcontracostahistory.org

Credits: Back cover photograph of Francis E. Donner Wilder with permission of Mark McLaughlin, Mic Mac Publishing.

Cover and interior design by Leigh McLellan Design, http://www.leighmcdesign.com

Every attempt has been made to verify the accuracy of the history herein. All errors and omissions are the responsibility of the editor.

Errata and updates to: ECCHS@EastContraCostaHistory.org

A publication of Byron Hot Springs
www.ByronHotSprings.com

www.ingramcontent.com/pod-product-compliance
Lightning Source LLC
Chambersburg PA
CBHW042002150426
43194CB00002B/100